CARVING RANGE

A GUIDE TO CARVING GOLF BALLS

by Justin Jepsen

Introduction 2
Evolution of Golf Balls 3
Carving Tools 6
Sharpening Techniques 8
Opening Golf Balls 11
Carving the Golf Balls.............. 15
    The Scoutmaster................ 16
    The Cowboy.................. 21
    The Boy 25
    The Baseball Manager............. 29
Painting the Carving............... 33
    The Scoutmaster................ 34
    The Boy 37
Sprucing Up the Carving 39
My Carving Gallery................ 41

INTRODUCTION

So you want to learn how to carve? Carving, or whittling, is a wonderful hobby which can open the door to many other artistic pursuits. A college professor for years introduced all of his students to a pocketknife and a piece of wood on their first day of class and the students were instructed to carve. When the students mastered the carving techniques they would proceed to learn other crafts. The professor found that the experience derived from carving would carry over to other crafts. If they were found struggling in a craft invariably they would return to carving to re-master the crafts. As I have taught and observed others I see that this fact is true in others as well as in myself. When I carve, creative thoughts come more easily than when I don't carve.

There are many reasons for this book. First, I believe golf balls are a fun medium to carve in. The face is already round so achieving facial depth is often easier to accomplish than on a flat piece of wood. Second, is because of the many misconceptions of what is inside of a golf ball. The most commonly asked questions are "Don't they have elastic bands inside?" or "how do you glue on that wooden face so perfectly?" Third, opening the outer shell of golf balls can be dangerous. There are safer ways in opening them and in explaining these ways many accidents may be eliminated. Most of all, carving golf balls is fun, unique and addicting. The rubber core is soft and nice to carve. The ball fits perfectly in ones hand and for all of the people who are so fascinated with carving they may pick up this book and have a momentary twinkle in their eye when they are taught step-by-step, with the hope that they too can carve well.

Carving for me is not for making the extra dollar but the developing of the individual. This focus is why I have and continue to develop talents. I hope that through carving you too can further develop your talents whether it is whittling, carving, or another artistic or creative aspect, thus enabling you to help develop the individual, be it be yourself or someone you touch.

Happy Carving! Justin Jepsen

EVOLUTION OF GOLF BALLS

A recent outside cover of a package of golf balls states, "The thin Titanium enhanced cover helps transfer the energy from the club for more distance. And it's cut-proof. A new softer high energy core gives this ball increased distance with a softer feel." Research for greater efficiency and performance, distance, feel and control has left golf balls with an interesting evolution.

Although this not a comprehensive history of the golf ball, it is a fun historical journey to take. First we journey back to 15th Century Europe where the first golf ball called the "Feathery" was introduced. The Feathery had a hand stitched leather cover with a stuffed core of goose or chicken feathers. When the final stitch was in place the Feathery was soaked in water, removed and finally dried. When dry, the feathers would expand and the leather would contract forming a solid ball. The Feathery was durable until it got wet. A downfall of the Feathery was that a good Feathery worker could only produce three or four Featheries a day.

The Feathery lasted until about 1848 when Reverend Adam Peterson of St. Andrews introduced the world to Gutta Percha. "Gutty," a rubber-like tree sap found in the gutta tree, was heated and fashioned into a ball. The Gutta Percha revolutionized the game of golf. They were more durable, more affordable, lasted longer, could be mass-produced, flew farther, and rolled truer on the greens. The Gutta Percha soon over took the Feathery. With greater ease in production more people entered the game of golf. With more people came the development of more courses and because people were hitting further the length between holes had to be increased.

The Gutta Percha continued to dominate golf, however golfers realized that the more nicks and scratches on the ball enhanced the aerodynamic performance. Soon metal molds were created to create similar bramble patterns on all Gutta Percha balls. The gutty sap was black so the early balls were painted white which enabled golfers to easily find their golf balls. Golfers could even buy touch up paint to spruce up the balls.

The Vardon Flyer, similar to the Gutta Percha was the first American made ball. It came and went with little success due to new ball technology. This development consisted of a rubber wound core with a gutty cover called the Haskell.

Coburn Haskell, a manufacturer at B.F. Goodrich Rubber Co., developed this rubber wound core with a gutty outside. This new ball flew farther but was met with some criticism and quickly received the nickname "Bounding Billies" because it was difficult to control. It was not until numerous tournament successes that the Haskell received player recognition.

In the early 1900's ball advances came rather quickly. Spalding, after having failed with the Vardon Flyer, introduced the Wizard. This was a rubber ball with a balata cover. The cover adhered to the rubber windings of the inner core better. Spalding also introduced the first "true" white balls rather than black balls painted white. In 1905 W. Taylor invented the first dimpled ball improving ball pattern. This pattern created maximum lift and minimum drag. Elazer Kempshall of the United States and Frank Mingay of Scotland experimented with liquid core balls. Other companies also experimented the sacs loaded with mixtures combining everything from water and lead to tapioca. By the 1920's the Gutta Perchas faded and the more effective balata cover replaced it. The dimple was the king and few changes were made during the next several years.

Golf ball changes came again after a dentist/golfer questioned the poor consistent ball performance. This dentist x-rayed several golf balls and he found several deformities and discrepancies of weight placement and he sought to make a perfectly round ball positioned around a core. The company he founded was Titlest. After World War II the game of golf soared because of an increase of rubber resources and leisure time. Experimentation continued to take place and the first commercially available golf ball with Dupont's tough-to-cut synthetic material Surlyn was introduced. Spalding came out with the first two-piece ball known as the Executive. This was a solid mass wrapped in Surlyn. It won acceptance because of the further flying distance.

Two and three piece balls kept improving, new synthetic materials were created and more dimples squeezed into the cover adding more distance and control. Dimples grew in number from 350 to 400 or 500. There were variations in the sizes and shapes of dimples. This variation of patterns affected a ball's flight, particularly in trajectory.

Competition and speculation continues on today as golf ball technology continues to soar onward and upward. In a world where manufactures continually push the limits seeking for a ball that flies farther and straighter without sacrificing control, it is questionable which golf ball is best for competition. In the early 1990's about 20% of competitors were using solid balls while the other 80% continued to use rubber wound balls. By the late 1990's that number had switched.

Today, golf balls come in two piece solid or three piece solid, rubber wound, double shell, or even a titanium enhanced cover. Ball technology will continue to thrive as the sport of golf continues to grow in popularity. For our purposes all we have to question is how easily does the cover come off and how well does it carve.

The centers of a golf ball range from elastic bands to solid cores.

SOURCES
From Hickory Cleeks to Metal Woods; James A. Fran,k pg 180-194
Golf for Dummies; Gary McCord, pg 17-18, 1999

CARVING TOOLS

There are many tools that may be used for carving golf balls. I primarily use a pocket knife or a bench knife, however, in smaller cuts I find that a small hand chisel or V-tool is very helpful. Many experts primarily use hand chisels, exacto knives, and some have even used small power tools for carving. For the purpose of this book we will discuss carving basics with a knife.

A knife is your primary asset and should be treated with care. In choosing a knife, you will want a knife of good quality. Quality knives are not necessarily expensive and a good one may be picked up in many stores. In years past it was recommend purchasing a knife of good carbon steel rather than a stainless steel. However, both have proven to be great for carving.

One of the best ways to find a knife is to pick it up. The feel of it is most important. You want it to fit comfortably in your hand and ask yourself, "Is it too heavy or too light?" Remember you want a knife that you can carve with for hours. A good pocketknife should have two or three blades. Any more will make it too bulky, heavy, and hard to handle. Other things you want to consider when purchasing a knife are what the blade's flexibility is and if it is a fixed blade.

We will use a bench knife. I like a bench knife because you can get a good quality blade at a relatively inexpensive price. Another benefit of a bench knife is the longer handle which gives more leverage and power in a cut. The knife blade is also fixed and won't close. The one I use is less than $20.00. I have assisted in teaching many classes to young people with pocket knives and fixed blades. When we went to the bench knife, fewer cuts resulted and the knives quit walking away.

After you have chosen a knife the most important and usually most difficult thing to carving is to keep your knife sharp. Sharpening knives will be further discussed in the next section but I can promise that you will have a more enjoyable time carving and stay with carving longer when your knife is sharp. More people are frustrated and don't carve because it is no fun when your knife is not working for you and that is "dull" for both you and the knife. One of the best ways to keep a knife sharp is to use the carving blade for carving only. Using a carving blade for cutting paper, sod, insulation, sandy surfaces or anything else destroys the blade alignment and makes the blade dull. Also keep a little oil in and on the knife, sweat from hands causes rust. Finally remember that time of non-use affects the edge of the knife blade.

Standard Carving Knives — Bench knives "Flex-cut" Brand - a detail knife (left) amd cutting knife (middle). Finally a four-blade Henckel pocket knife. The blades shown on the pocketknife are similar to those on the bench knives.

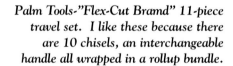

Palm Tools-"Flex-Cut Bramd" 11-piece travel set. I like these because there are 10 chisels, an interchangeable handle all wrapped in a rollup bundle.

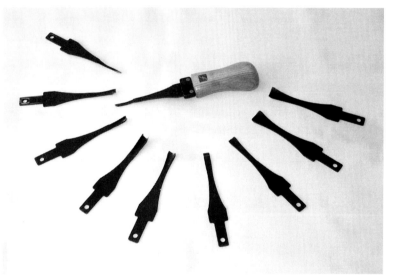

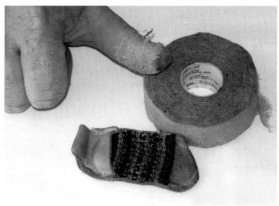

Thumb guard and High Friction Safety Tape. Although it is not necessary to use one, these are good to put on the thumb to cut down on the minor cuts. Both are very good. I used the thumb guard for a long time but found that the safety tape works very well. It offers a lot truer feeling in the thumb.

SHARPENING TECHNIQUES

You sharpen a knife in stages starting with a coarse stone and moving to a medium then a fine stone and finally completing the process with a leather strop. All knives come with a manufactures edge or bevel approximately 35°-45°. For most carving you will want to rework the blade angle of the knife to 10° or less. Reworking the bevel will allow the knife the cut better and remain sharper for longer amounts of time when carving. Once you have a carving angle on your blade rarely will you have to resharpen it on a coarse stone unless you drop it or nick it somehow. The strop will take care of any fine tuning. Stropping is the process of fine tuning your blade. Sharpening the knife will create a burr along the edge. Stropping will remove the burr and leave the knife shiny. Be aware that sharpening does take time and that it is beneficial to learn how to correctly sharpen a knife. The duration of your involvement in carving will directly be linked to the ability to learn how to keep tools sharp. Just remember sharpening takes time and patience.

Sharpening Stones — DMT Diamond Stones and Natural stones. Stones come in all different kinds each one works and each has their pluses and minuses. I have found that someone can have a whet stone and keep his or her tools just as sharp as someone with a diamond stone. Natural stones are more economical, in buying a natural stone you have to decide if it will be a water or oil stone. If you decide to make the stone an oil you can not change back to a water stone. Be careful with new sharpening gimmick's a person thinking that the whet stone is the reason for not being able to sharpen and purchases a diamond stone will still only be happy if they learn to sharpen correctly.

Strops—both of these are hand made strops, with jewelers rouge or fine abrasive grit. You can purchase strops or make your own. These are made with a piece of leather glued on a flat board, the kind of leather doesn't really matter and the board is just something you can tote around. The advantage of the board is when working a blade it leaves a flat edge on the blade rather than a wavy edge.

Sharpening Procedure: lay the knife blade against the stone. Slant the blade on the edge of a quarter to determine the angle of the blade. In a cutting motion, making sure to get the full blade, bring the blade forward across the stone. Continue to work the blade on this coarse stone making sure that you get the entire blade each time through.

To strop, place the knife blade on the side of leather with the abrasive grit. Drag the blade back in opposite direction of a cut. Continue dragging the blade the full length of the leather for five to ten strokes then switch to the other side of the blade.

Turn the blade over and do the same to this side of the blade. Every time, be sure to watch your angle. When you feel you have reworked the bevel, proceed to a medium stone. Use the same steps on the medium and fine stones as with the coarse stone; bringing the knife blade back and forth against the stone. Ideally the only time you should ever have to use a coarse and medium stone is the first time sharpening unless you drop the knife or want to rework the blade angle. Most of the sharpness will come with the fine stone and the strop.

Strop the same way on the other side, the same amount of times. Continue switching back and forth between sides until you have a sharp blade. Stropping has to be consistent. Just like in sharpening keep the same angle each time.

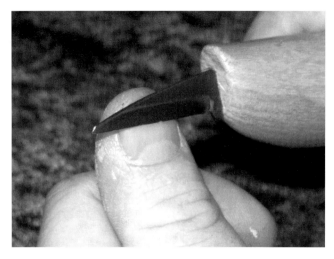

You can check blade sharpness by running the blade down the fingernail toward the cuticle. If it grabs the blade is sharp. If not the blade is dull. The sharper the knife the more easily it will grab. Make sure you check this along the full blade. You may find the middle and tip to be sharp but the bottom of the blade dull. If this is the case the blade requires a little more work. *Remember there is no time lost in sharpening it always pays off.*

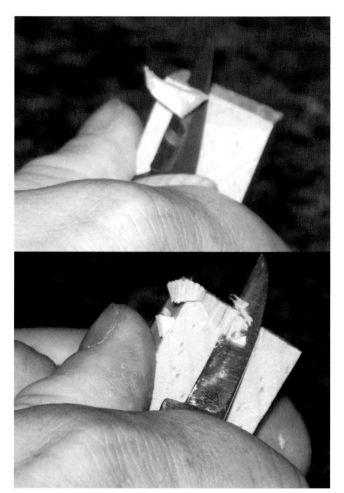

Another way to check blade sharpness is to cut wood cross grain as in the diagram. The top shows a smooth clean cut with a sharp knife. The example on the bottom is a dull knife, which breaks and hacks away at the wood leaving a shabby cut.

Hand Chisels have varying techniques to sharpening each chisel. Once the technique of sharpening a knife is mastered, chisels are very similar to that of a knife. We will not cover sharpening hand chisels. If using a chisel seek out and learn those techniques to make carving more enjoyable.

Remember, very few tools are more dangerous than a dull knife. Sharpness adds to the overall safety and enjoyment of carving. Sharp knives reduce cutting force required which equals more control. Less control equals more force and faster tiring. A sharp knife will produce a cleaner cut and add overall to a finished carving. I cannot over emphasis the importance of sharp tools.

OPENING GOLF BALLS

In the chapter "Evolution of Golf Balls" a statement was made referring to the cover of the titanium golf ball. It said, "…and it's cut proof." I add my statement from when I first began carving golf balls, "I don't think golf balls were made to get into." However, since then experimentation has cracked the shell. In golf ball carving you need to decide whether to purchase pre-opened golf balls or to open them yourself. I realize that many people will question buying pre-opened golf balls when they have a bucket full of golf balls in the basement crying out their name to redeem them from their outer shell. Still there are differences.

PRE-OPENED GOLF BALLS–There is a company* that pre-open's brand new golf balls that come with a clean cut as well as the disregarded half of the shell still intact. It is 100% safe and there is no guessing as to what is inside the ball.

OPENING YOUR OWN GOLF BALLS–The hardest thing about opening your own golf balls is the inconsistencies you discover. You'll find that some are so solid that it is too difficult to carve, some have elastic bands, and some even have double shells making it nearly impossible to open. With those golf balls in the basement, golf balls purchased from the five and dime or from pawnshops you just don't know what you'll find. You will just have to take your chances. When purchasing new golf balls read the outer cover looking for two piece golf balls made with surlyn or a solid core.

*Treeline: www.treelineusa.com

75% of the golf balls, 5 years or newer, will have solid rubber cores. It is difficult to find consistent inner cores. A person could buy a sleeve of golf balls and find different colors, hardness, and even toxicity. In deciding what to use, keep these questions in mind to help determine whether you should purchase pre-opened golf balls or open them yourself.

- What is available and what am I willing to pay for it?
- Where will it be used or displayed?
- Will it be painted?
- Is this just for practice?

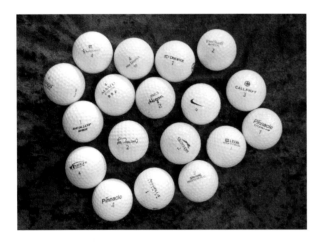

OPENING YOUR OWN GOLF BALLS

#1 **Be Careful** whatever you do! Make sure to wear protective safety glasses. I will introduce two techniques with variations. Whether you use one of these techniques or another way, remember to be careful.

LATHE–I like the lathe and find it a safe, fast, and clean way to open golf balls. However, I realize not everybody has access to a lathe.

Place the golf ball in the lathe. Use the drive center on one end and a faceplate on the other end. There has to be enough pressure to hold the ball snug in place. The drive center creates a small hole in one end that is not a problem because it will be the discarded shell. You can make your own set up using chucks or wooden blocks.

REMOVING TOP

Tighten the golf ball in place as well as the tool rest.

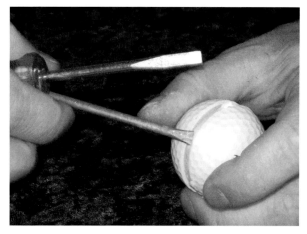

Take a screwdriver and wedge the blade under the cover of the half that will be discarded.

I use a Wood Turning Skew, but any skew will do. A parting tool also works however it cuts a wider gap. Apply enough pressure so your skew doesn't wander. Another alternative to a skew is using a hacksaw.

Take a second screw driver and wedge the blade under the cover next to the first.

Identify when you have gone far enough by noticing a change of colors in the cut or by feeling a different texture. Once you have cut through either remove the golf ball from the lathe or you may leave the ball clamped in the lathe for opening.

Continue to slide the blade under the cover until the top comes off. You will feel the shell release the pressure.

PADDED VICE–The padded vice is a little slower than the lathe yet much more economical to use if you don't have a lathe.

With the padded vice you'll want to draw a centerline before opening. To draw the center line use a plumbers gasket, a fitted piece of paper cut at 13/16" high, or drill a 1-5/8" hole in a piece of 1/8" plywood and drop the ball inside the hole. Use anything that will make a straight line. With a permanent marker draw a line around the ball. Permanent marker will easily come off with alcohol or acetone. Remember to know where the brand name is for the back of the golf ball.

Clamp the ball in a padded vice with the centerline facing up.

Take an 18-tooth hack saw and begin cutting through the shell. The hack saw allows you to feel when you have reached the rubber core. Continue as far as you can in this position, then unclamp the ball, rotate, and continue around the entire ball. Remove cover as shown on the previous page. Another method in place of hacksaw is to use thin grinding wheels on a power tool such as a Dremmel.

A few more thoughts on golf balls and safety. Some balls do have some toxicity associated with them. The toxicity adds to the softness of the ball and therefore creates a greater ease in carving them. Toxicity is a double edged sword. You want to keep them soft yet you don't want to get sick from the smell. To keep the toxicity don't remove the cover of too many balls too long before carving them. It also helps to keep opened balls in a sealed container; a plastic bag will do. When whittling, do so in a well ventilated area which will eliminate most problems. Finally, remember golf balls come in a variety of colors, toxicites, and densities. When opening golf balls remember to be smart. Some ways of opening golf balls are just plain stupid so don't try them. You will find golf balls that have rubber bands, liquid cores, smell bad, and even shoot all over. This is all part of the fun.

CARVING THE GOLF BALLS

The projects I have chosen reflect the most commonly asked for styles as well as others I've completed. With a combination of any of the four carvings, you should be able to accomplish any of the carvings in the gallery. For example, carving a Santa Claus requires a similar hat to that of the Flat Hat and mustache and beard carvings from the Cowboy. The projects take you from beginners to more advanced styles and will require some work for total mastery. I have been carving for many years and I still learn new things. You will learn how to make a smiling and frowning faces, teeth as well as a mustache and a beard. The hair on a boy can easily be used on a girl although girls are rarely made because of the crude features of charicatures. Carving is a fun hobby, which does not require much in the way of overhead or tools. Most carvings can be completed in under an hour while a sculpture can take weeks, months or even years thus frustrating beginners. The carving steps will read down the left column first and then the right column of each page.

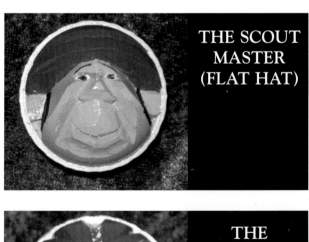

THE SCOUT MASTER (FLAT HAT)

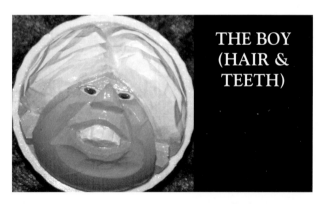

THE BOY (HAIR & TEETH)

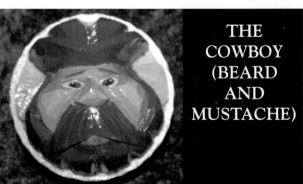

THE COWBOY (BEARD AND MUSTACHE)

THE BASEBALL MANAGER (BALL CAP)

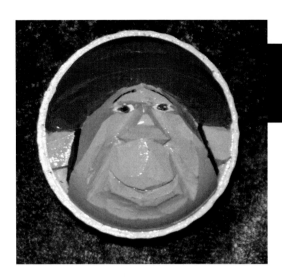

CARVING THE SCOUT MASTER (FLAT HAT)

I start with the Flat Hat because I feel it is the easiest type of cap to start with.

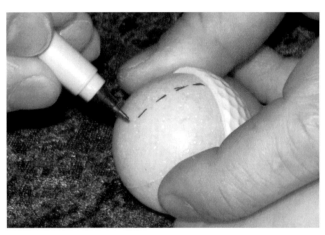

Begin with making a dotted centerline from the top to the bottom and from left to right. Make sure to see what is on the reverse of the ball, is the right side up not sideways or upside down.

Make a line coming from the left centerline arching in the middle and ending at the right centerline, this will be the bottom of brim of the Flat Hat. Drawing a line is important in beginning carving to show where one is going. Also it's important in golf ball carving because the material is very forgiving and it is hard to see where you made a previous cut. The greater the arch in the dotted line will determine the slope of the hat.

The center line is important because that will be the ridge of the nose as well as the general area for all other lines.

Hold the golf ball in your hand, opposite the hand you will carve with. The dotted line we identified as the bottom brim is where you'll make your first cut. Cut straight in, not too far, but enough to make a stopper cut. A Stopper cut is a cut you make first before carving up into that cut. In theory the cut should stop the blade from traveling farther than the initial cut.

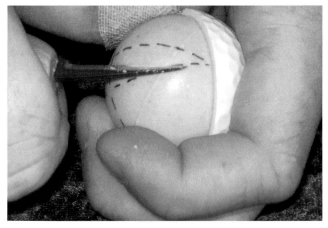

Once you have made a stopper cut around the entire brim, cut at a diagonal from the center line up to the stopper cut.

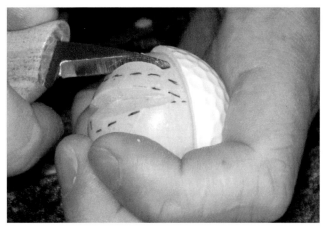

Then make a diagonal cut back towards that cut.

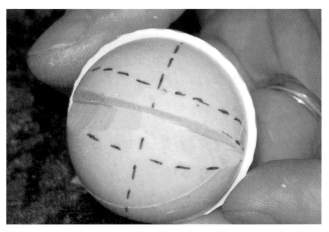

Continue to do this on all sides, this will remove the first parts of the golf ball. You should get something like this with the upper part being the brim of the hat and the nose ridge in the middle. I have also added an additional dotted line for the top of the hat. Allow the width between lower and upper brim to be plenty wide. This will prevent breaking the brim. It can be tapered down in the end.

Finally make a mark for the corners of the hat and notch the piece out.

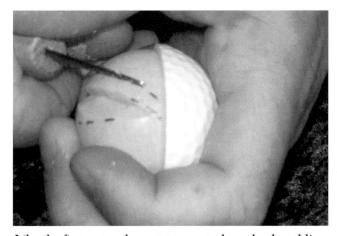

Like the first cut make a stopper cut along the dotted line.

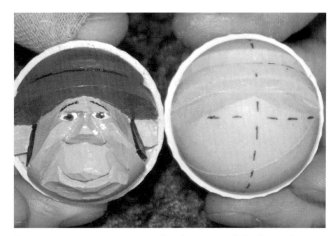

In comparison we can see the features of the hat, the hat is finished for now. We can return and clean up later if there is a need.

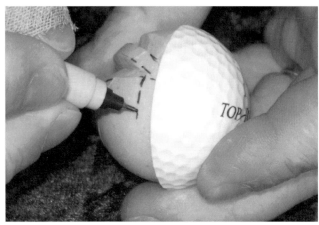

On both sides make a dotted line from the brim of the hat parallel with the edge of golf ball, this will be the mark for the ears. Like the hat, over exaggerate a little for the ears. They are easier to cut down than to put back.

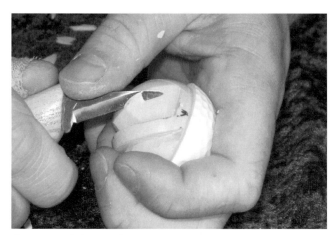

Continue defining the ears and nose ridge by cutting towards the brim tapering out at the center.

Make a stopper cut straight back on the ears.

You can see the brim as well as the nose ridge and the ears on both sides. I like to look at the bottom view because it shows if I am still on center. If not, you can trim down one side or the other.

Cut back diagonally toward the stopper cut.

A front view, add a dotted line for the brow.

Make a stopper cut for the brow.

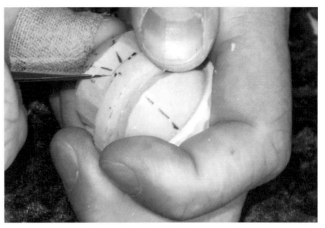

Cut in nose and cheeks by making a stopper cut and then making a cut back into itself.

Cut back diagonally towards the brow.

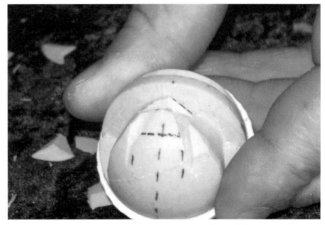

See the cuts we just made. Make a dotted line at the base of the nose. Cut down on the dotted line and then come back towards it with a diagonal cut.

We want to create cheeks coming from the middle of the brow leading out like the side of a triangle coming down with a dotted line on each side.

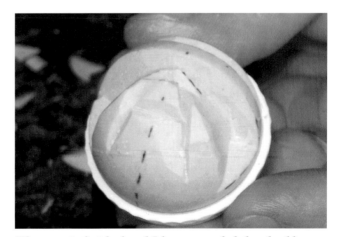

The nose is finished and I have extended the cheekbone a little further as well as cleaned and rounded the side. Continue to round getting ready for the mouth.

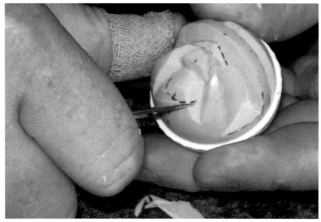

For a smile draw in with a dotted line. Follow the line around with the tip of the knife blade, but not too deep. Re-trace the mouth with the tip of the blade using a diagonal cut a little higher up, taking out the middle section of the mouth.

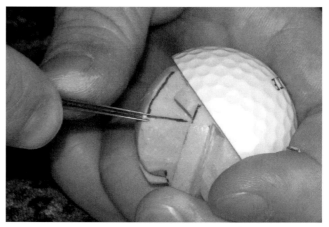

Draw in side burns; either use a knife or use a small V-tool to carve out the line, just follow the line around.

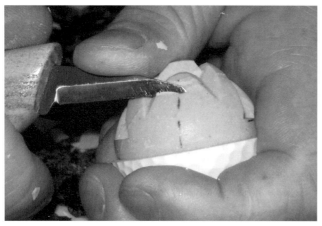

To further define the lower lip notch out a small sliver on the bottom of the lip.

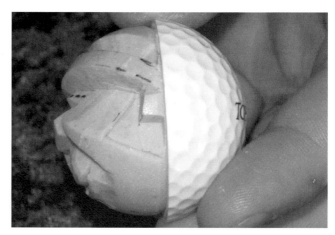

Finish of the side burns.

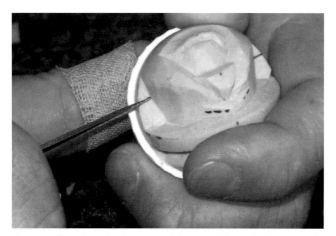

Draw a line for the bottom of the ear lobs; the bottom of the ear should be the same line as the bottom of the nose. Cut down along the line, then in from the back and down along the face removing the piece.

Comparison of the finished carving.

THE COWBOY (BEARDS AND MUSTACHES)

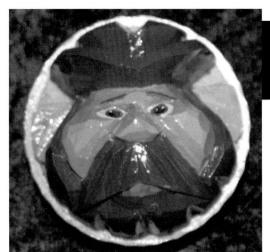

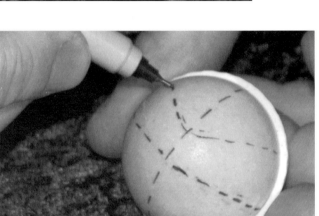

Make the center lines, then a V-line for the Cowboy hat starting at the centerline and slanting upwards. The line will determine the slant of the hat.

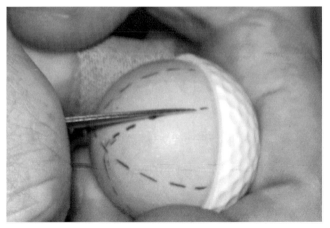

Follow dotted line around with a stopper cut.

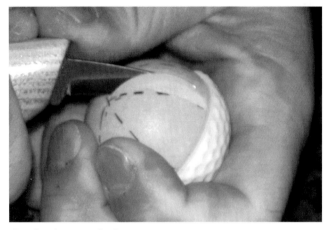

Cut back towards the stopper cut.

Continue cutting away at the lower brim and then add the upper brim line.

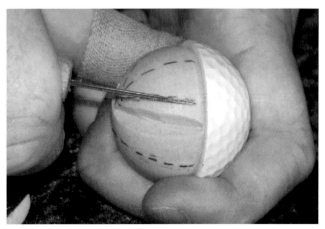

Cut away as did before making a stopper cut and cutting back to that cut.

Notch a V in the top of the hat adding definition.

Carve back towards the stopper cut on both sides then begin to round up to the brim.

Comparison of the Cowboy hat.

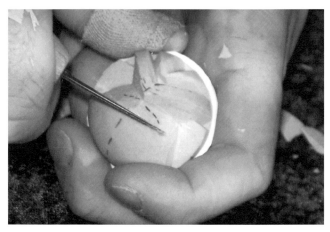

Draw in the brow line, make a diagonal cut and cut back towards itself.

Draw in a dotted line for the ears and cut straight back making a stopper cut.

Make triangular lines for nose, mustache and cheeks, it is all the same line.

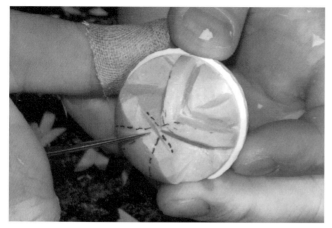

Make a stopper cut one lines and cut along both sides.

Draw lines for mustache and follow it around with tip of blade as with the smile in the Flat Hat. Then follow the line back around.

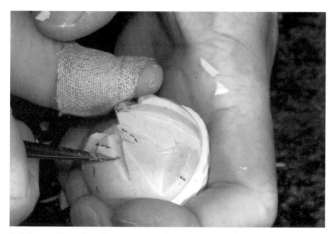

Make a line for the nose and cut a straight stopper cut then follow it back up towards the nose.

Draw in the lower lip. You can see how the mustache shows up. Follow the mouth around with knife then cut a diamond out of the top of the mustache.

Start rounding the mustache and extend the mustache line a little.

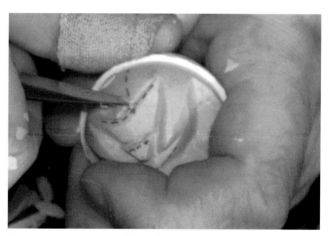

Round bottom of the lip.

This is where you would stop if you wanted only a mustache. If you desire to stop here add in sideburns and even up ears like in the Flat Hat.

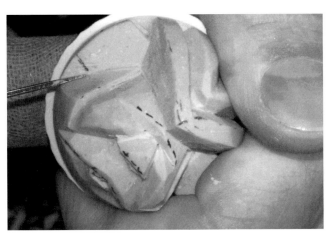

Make a line for the ears and trim off the ears at top and bottom of the line.

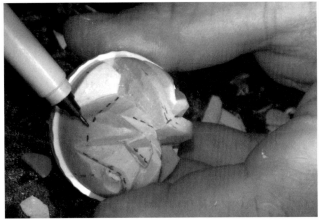

Draw a line for the beard extending the side burns down along the edge of the mustache.

Follow the mustache and beard lines with V-tool or a knife.

Make your straight stopper cut along the line, cut back in to the stopper cut.

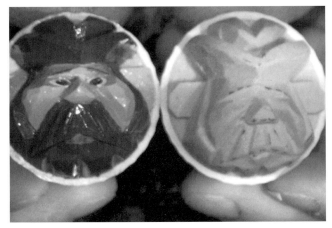

Comparison of the finished Cowboy.

CARVING THE BOY (HAIR & TEETH)

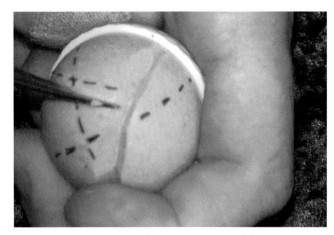

Cut all the way across the hair. This will be the parted side. Then begin to cut on the other side.

Draw centerlines followed by the hairlines.

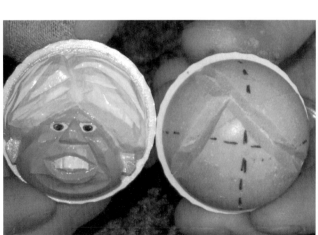

Comparing the hair.

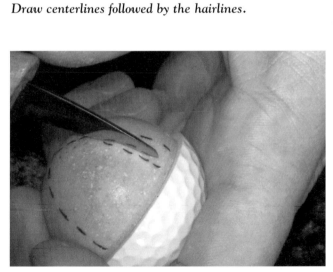

Cut down along the hair dotted line making a stopper cut then cutting back up into the stopper cut.

Cut towards the hair creating the nose ridge in the center of the ball. You can see that the part in the hair is a little to the side.

Draw in the ears. With a straight stopper cut, begin to trim the ears out.

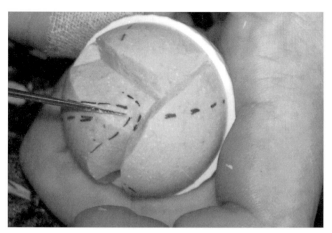

Make the nose and cheek lines and cut them out.

You can see now how the ears are in place. Add in the dotted line for the brow.

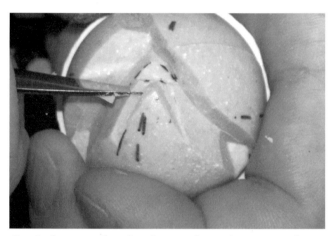

Cut little eye sockets by shaving down the area so the eyes will be flush with the nose. If you do not even them up they will often appear to be looking up rather than out.

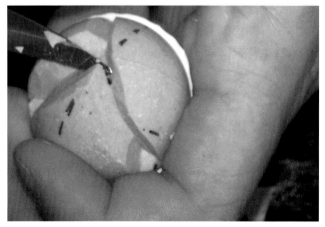

Make your stopper cut at the brow than cut up towards the brow.

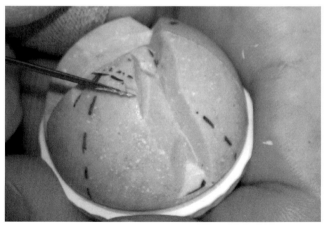

Make the nose line, then a stopper cut along that line.

How does he look?

Draw in the upper lip, then follow the line around as in the lower lip.

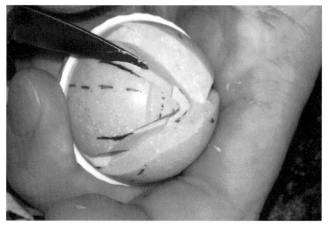

Extend the cheek a little and round the lips as in the past carvings.

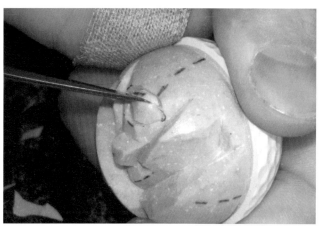

Straigthen up the teeth by shaving the teeth flat towards the upper lip.

Draw in a smiley face as in the Flat Hat but this time draw it just a little lower so we can fit in the teeth. Cut out the smile.

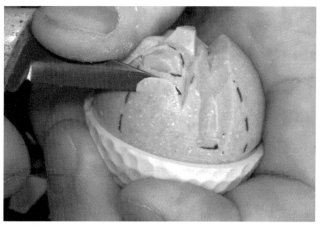

Round the lower for lip definition.

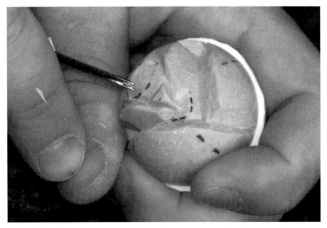

Take a small hand chisel or knife to make the teeth.

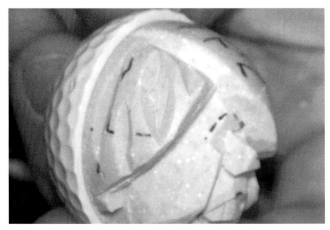

Use a V-tool or knife to cut out the creases in the hair.

Cut the ears down to the base of the nose.

Comparision of the finished product.

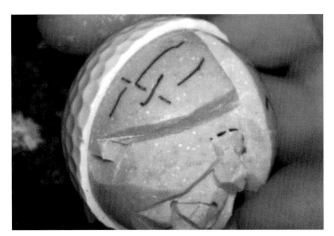

Make some hair lines.

THE BASEBALL MANAGER (THE BALL CAP)

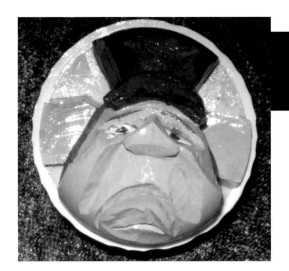

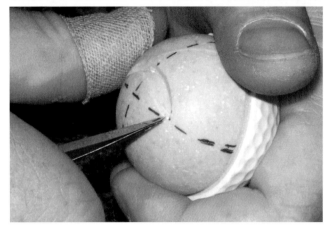

Next cut away along the center line and up towards the brim. Continue to cut and clean out.

Begin with centerlines then a half circle rising up from the centerline. This will be the ball cap brim.

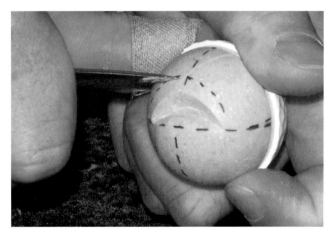

Draw upper brim and follow the line and make sure to follow at a diagonal or you could cut right through the brim.

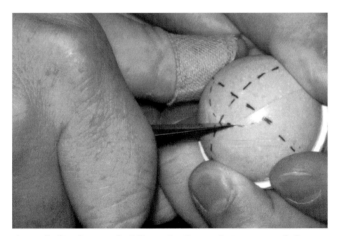

At a slight diagonal, follow the lower brim around the dotted line. The more diagonal the cut, the steeper the brim. Remember don't force the cut.

Draw in the top of the hat. Cut straight back and be careful not to force away cut.

Working towards the hat, the back should be flush with golf ball.

You can get the cap to appear more like a ball cap by drawing a line from the tip of the cap to its base and making cuts back towards the cap.

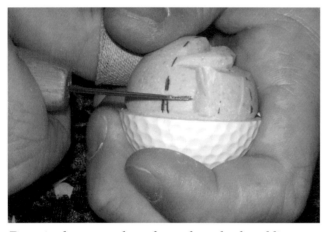

Draw in the ears and cut down along the dotted line.

Draw a line extending out from cap to shape the brim.

Continue bringing the ears back in toward hat.

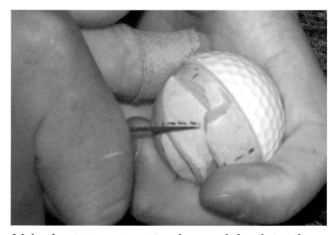

Make the stopper cut cutting down and then bring the other cut into the stopper cut.

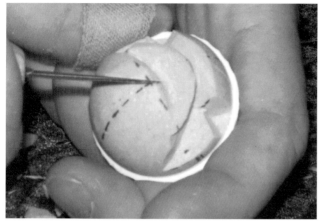

From the middle line cut back to the brim creating the nose ridge.

With the hat down, make your cut along the line for the stopper cut and cut back towards it for the cheeks.

Make a brow line following the angle of the hat and make your downward stopper cut.

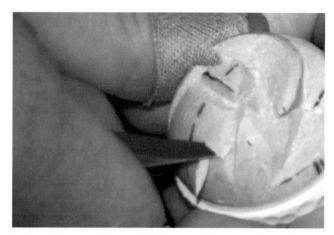

I have drawn a line at the bottom of nose and cut the nose at the base. Proceed to extend cheeks and round the mouth area.

Make triangular lines for the cheeks and nose.

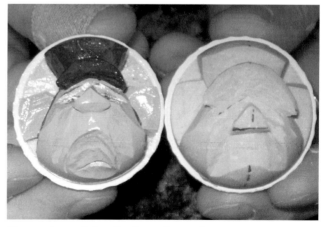

Comparison of the cheeks and mouth.

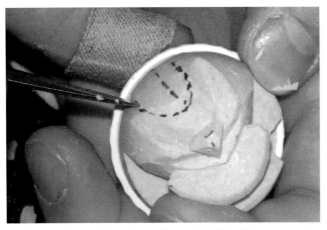

A frowny face is like the smile on the Flat Hat except it is upside down. Draw in lines and follow it around with tip then follow it around again just a bit higher.

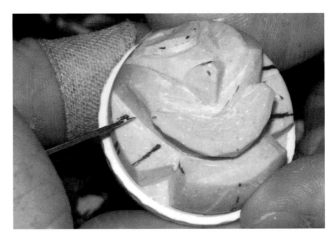

Define the ears at the base of nose and close to the tip of the nose. Cut along the line.

To create the lip, slightly round the bottom of the frown.

Side burns with a little hair. Again use a V-tool or knife to cut out.

To make a facial dimple or swell cliff follow the V mark around like the mouth.

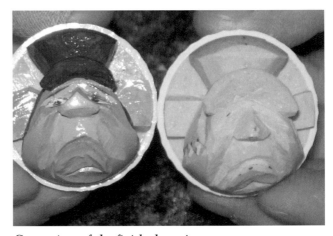

Comparison of the finished carving.

PAINTING THE CARVING

Colors of Paints: Purchase a medium flesh tone, white, black, primary colors; red, yellow, and blue. I also use a brown and a green.

Nothing can make a project better than a little paint and varnish after the task of carving is over. My least favorite part of golf ball art is finishing up but a good paint job is more than half of the battle when it comes to carving golf balls.

Use a water-based acrylic paint because they dry quickly and the colors are very easy to blend. I have tried many other paints because water-based acrylic does not adhere as well to the surface as I would like, but all others have their own downfalls. Model oil paints are hard to blend and don't come in very many colors. For example, it is difficult to blend the colors of fire engine red and jet black. Oil based are very toxic and dry quickly. I find the best paint to use is a water based acrylic paint.

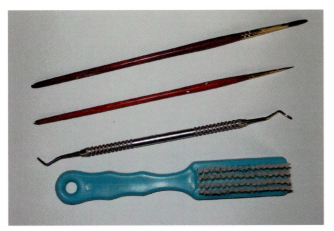

Preparation and Painting—the top two are paint brushes. I like to use a little higher quality paint brush. It seems to work a little better and the bristles stay in place longer. I figure in the long run an expensive brush will cost the same amount as two or three cheap brushes. I also like to use dentist pick to clean up the paint around the outside of the golf ball. Finally, a stiff brush can clean away any loose chips that may still be holding onto the golf ball.

A cup of water and a plastic palette. The success of painting will come in using plenty of water to even out the paint on the surface of the golf ball.

PAINTING THE SCOUTMASTER

Before painting take a coarse brush and rub across the surface of the golf ball. This will clean any loose chips or burrs away. If further finishing needs to be done now is the time to do it for it is easier when not painted.

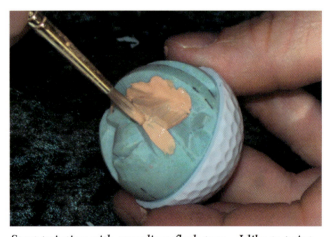

Start painting with a medium flesh tone. I like to paint with a large brush not worrying about what paint gets where quite yet. Make sure to use plenty of water making the paint blend smoothly.

While the paint is still wet blend in a little brown or red to accentuate the eye area as well as the mouth, cheeks and ears this creates a good base color.

Remember to paint the ears.

Paint the hat. Once again use the large brush for the major areas

With closer detail near the base of the hat begin to use a smaller brush.

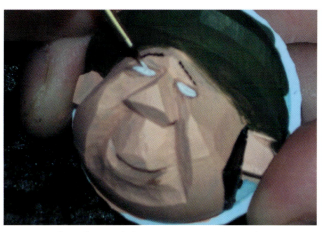

Paint in the whites of the eyes. Try and get them as similar as possible. (See step 2 of the eye chart)

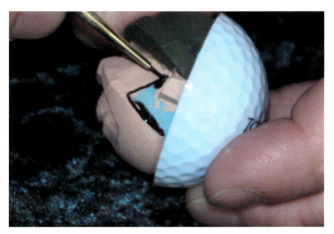

With fine brush, outline the side burns then fill in.

Add the color to the eyes by making a filled in circle. (See step 3 of the Eye Chart)

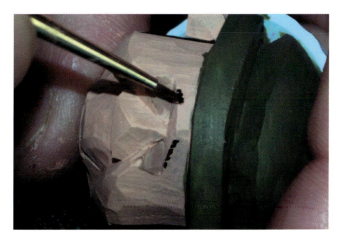

Get any globs of paint off the fine brush. Paint in the eyebrows.

On top of the green eye make a smaller circle of black. (See Step 4 of the Eye Chart)

E Y E   C H A R T

1 2 3 4 5

Finally add a speck of white, the glimmer of the eye. (See Step 5 of the Eye Chart)

The finished product, ready for the next step of sprucing up.

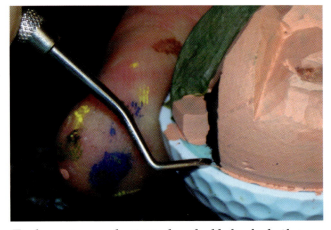

To clean up use a dentist tool or the blade of a knife to remove excess paint around the edges.

PAINTING THE BOY

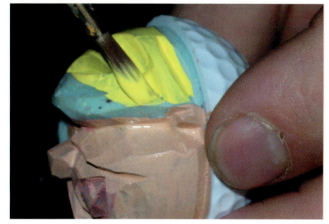

A free spirit like this kid has to have yellow hair.

Paint face with medium flesh tone.

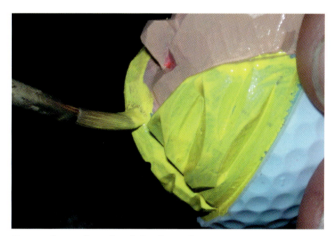

Paint the underside of the hair also.

Blend in red to the eyes and mouth to add depth and contrast.

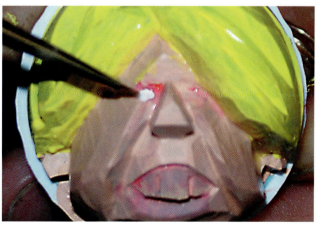

Paint in the eyebrows with a hint of brown. Next, paint the whites of the eyes in an oval shape.

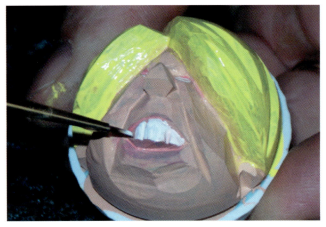
While your brush has white on it paint the teeth.

Paint in a dab of black.

In painting the teeth don't paint teeth all the way back in the mouth, this makes the teeth look too full.

Top off the eye with a white dot for that sparkle in his eye.

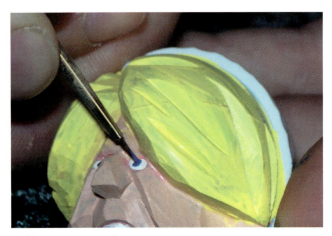
Add in your eye color.

Clean-up with a dental tool or knife for the finished carving.

SPRUCING UP THE CARVING

Now that you have finished your carving and painted it, now what? The possibilities are really endless, but in this section I will show two of the most popular things I have done to spruce up my finished carvings and make them truly unique and more enjoyable.

Spray gloss available at any craft store enhances the color of the carving while providing a protective coating.

Both projects requre a little drilling to get started. Use a 9/64-inch drill bit. For the stand, you need to drill a hole in the discarded half of the golf ball cover. For bolo ties, drill a hole in the top of two golf tees. (Below) To finish the stand, I insert a two inch golf tee in the hole I drilled in the cover, then place the carving on the stand.

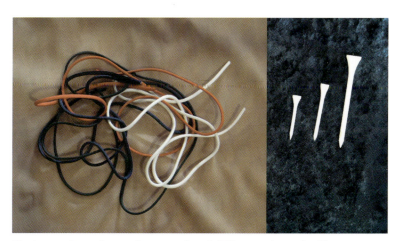

Spray a light coating over the top of the painted balls. I like to use an old egg carton to hold them in place while I spray.

Various colors of parachute cord and different sizes of golf tees can be used to make a bolo tie. Golf tees can also be used to create unique display stands.

39

For the bolo tie, a little additional drilling is required. Use a 3/16-inch bit. This is best accomplished using a drill press. To avoid damaging your paint job, you may want to drill before painting your carving.

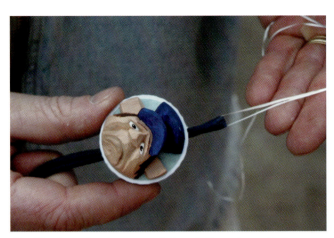

Feed both ends of a piece of dental floss through the bottom hole. Loop the parachute cord through the dental floss and then pull through. For leverage, twist the dental floss around a pen or piece of wood.

If you find the bit wanders from a straight path, drill halfway in the top, then turn the carving over and drill the other half from the bottom. Make sure you align the two holes so they meet.

When you have finished, you should have a bolo tie like this.

Glue each end of the parachute cord into the hole drilled in the top of each golf tee. Use epoxy or super glue. I find 48 icnes is a good length of parachute cord for a bolo tie.

Create trophies, Christmas ornaments, or displays to show off your carvings. I like to use a red golf tee with white pinstriping for the Santa Clause tee stand. You can find a variety of colored golf tees to use. Most importantly, make your carvings a piece of yourself.

MY CARVING GALLERY

I have provided this section to help "drive" your carving creativity. Use it as your carving 9 iron to come up with your own ideas for a carving gallery. Be creative and explore the endless possibilities of carving and of the novelties of golf. At the very end of the gallery, I have placed a photo showing the variety of colors found inside the golf balls.

The Carving Range

SAND TRAP MAN

THE CLASS CLOWN

YOUNG BALDY

YUKON

UNCLE SAND TRAP

OLD BALDY

HOLE, HOLE, HOLE

SANTA

HOLE SAINT NICK

Tex

Smokey

Hoss

Red Baron

Flight

Ace

Baden

Scout Master

Cubby

43

"Sport"

Dopey

Grumpy

Ole' Bucktooth

Scout

Water Boy

Line Backer

Quarter Back

Old Maid

44

Chief

Stinky

Safari Harry

Black Beard

Ahole Matey

Cheetah

Ms. Putter

Court Jester

Blondie

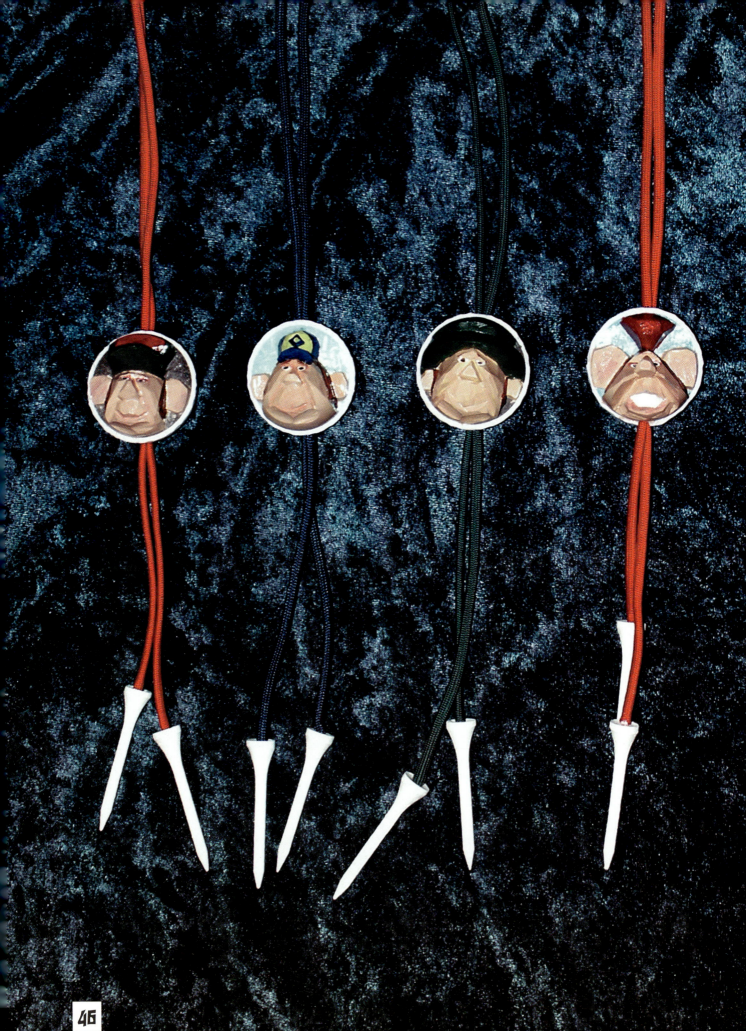